GLORIA
Triumph Over Adversity

Gloria Jean Thomas

Copyright Gloria Jean Thomas, 2024. All rights reserved.

This publication is designed to provide competent and reliable information regarding the subject matter. However, it is sold with the understanding that the author and publisher are not engaged in rendering legal, financial, or other professional advice. Laws and practices often vary from state to state, and if legal or other expert assistance is required, competent professionals should be sought. The author and publisher expressly disclaim any liability incurred from the use or application of the contents of this book.

Although based on true stories, certain events in the book have been fictionalized for educational content and impact. All rights reserved. No part of this book may be reproduced or transmitted in any form or by any means, electronic or mechanical, including photocopying, recording, or any information storage or retrieval system, without the publisher's written permission, except where permitted by law.

Cover design and photography: Xie "Maxine" Guiliane

Publisher: GGJTMinistry LLC

Publishing Assistant: Chief Empowerment Network, LLC

Editors: Dr. Roderick C. Cunningham, Valerie Cunningham, Erika Wyckoff, and Charmaigne Sering

ISBN: 9798-3004-4921-6

Printed in the United States of America

Dedication

This book is dedicated to all who have stumbled and fallen along the path of life but have found the strength to rise again. It is dedicated to those who have endured the darkest nights yet held fast to the promise of a new dawn.

To my son, who has taught me the true meaning of forgiveness and resilience. Your journey has inspired me more than words can express, and this book is a testament to the power of healing and reconciliation between us.

I am eternally grateful to my husband, whose love and unwavering faith have been my sanctuary. You have shown me the grace of God in human form.

My church family and spiritual mentors who have guided me with wisdom and patience, nurturing my growth in faith and spirit.

May this book be a beacon of hope and a source of encouragement for all who read it, reminding us that transformation is always possible with faith, perseverance, and love.

About the Author

Gloria Jean Hobbs-Thomas, born and raised in the humble community of Cedar Hammock, Florida, is a living testament to the power of faith and resilience. After enduring a tumultuous childhood marked by abuse, neglect, and a myriad of hardships, Gloria found solace and redemption through her unwavering faith in God.

Despite dropping out of school after the ninth grade and facing numerous personal and spiritual battles, Gloria's life transformed when she embraced her relationship with Jesus Christ. Her profound spiritual journey inspired her to help others overcome their struggles by sharing her recovery story and divine grace.

Gloria has dedicated her life to serving her community, ministering to those in need, and spreading a message of hope and forgiveness. She is an active member of her local church, serving in various capacities, including teaching Sunday school and participating in outreach programs. Her passion for food and communal gatherings is another avenue through which she expresses her love and care for people.

Her memoir is not just a recount of her past but a beacon of hope for anyone facing adversity. Gloria's mission is to show that transformation is possible through faith and perseverance, no matter one's beginnings or the depth of their despair.

Today, Gloria lives a fulfilled life with her husband, whom she affectionately calls "Honey," surrounded by a large and loving family that includes children, grandchildren, and great-grandchildren. She continues to write, speak, and share her life's lessons, driven by a desire to uplift and inspire. Her story is one of triumph over tragedy, a narrative she hopes will encourage others to seek healing and pursue a life marked by spiritual growth and service.

Table of Contents

Dedication iii
About the Author iv
Table of Contents vi
Acknowledgments vii
About the Book x
Introduction - The Dawn of Hope xii
Chapter 1 - The Seeds of Turmoil 1
Chapter 2 - Lost Innocence 11
Chapter 3 - The Struggle for Acceptance 19
Chapter 4 - In the Arms of False Saviors 27
Chapter 5 - The Spiral into Darkness 35
Chapter 6 - A Glimmer of Light 47
Chapter 7 - The Path to Healing Begins 61
Chapter 8 - Reclaiming My Life Through Faith and Forgiveness. 77
Chapter 9 - Love Rediscovered 97
Chapter 10 - A New Horizon 107
Chapter 11 - A Love Letter to My Legacy 115
CONCLUSION 119

Acknowledgments

First and foremost, I thank God, who has been my refuge and strength, a very present help in times of trouble. Without His unwavering grace and mercy, the journey of my life and the completion of this book would not have been possible.

To my beloved husband, your love and support have been my anchor through the storms and sunshine of life. Every moment with you has been a testament to God's grace. Your encouragement and unwavering companionship have enriched my journey immeasurably.

To my son, Mark Brown, firstly, I feel compelled to acknowledge the hurt I caused you publicly. Mark, I sincerely apologize for the pain brought into your life by my repeated mistakes and shortcomings as your mother. I ask that you please forgive me so that we can continue to break down any barriers that exist between us. With the time that God continues to grant us together, I am fully committed to pouring into the continued improvement of our relationship. From the bottom of my heart, thank you for walking this journey with me. You have witnessed my darkest days and, more recently, my brightest moments. I will forever treasure your love and the forgiveness that you have already granted. I know as we continue to work through the traumatic moments from your upbringing, there will be more for which I need to apologize. I love you unconditionally, and the bond we continue building means more to me than I can express.

To my stepchildren, Mike, Cedrick, Michael, and Michelle, I would also like to apologize for the damage I have caused you. I humbly ask for your forgiveness. I love you all unconditionally.

To Marcia and Bell, the mothers of my stepchildren, I ask that you forgive my irresponsible behavior and the role I failed to fulfill in our shared lives and parenting responsibly.

To my ex-husband Michael, please forgive me for my role in the pain and turmoil we inflicted on each other. 2 Corinthians 5:17 resonates deeply with me: "Therefore, if anyone is in Christ, he is a new creation; old things have passed away; behold, all things have become new."

I give special thanks to the Cusseaux family, especially Sherryl. Your support and unrelenting words of inspiration brought me immense encouragement when it was needed sorely. Your words resonate with me and have been a source of strength in my life. You could see the potential for my life long before it became evident to me. You believed in me even when a better future for myself seemed distant. Your faith in my abilities and prayers over my life pushed me to elevate and press harder toward my goals. I am eternally grateful for the immeasurable impact that your support and the support of your family have had on my life.

I sincerely thank my publishers, Rod and Valerie Cunningham, at Chief Empowerment Network, LLC. Their guidance and belief in my story have been invaluable, and I am deeply thankful for their patience, wisdom, and encouragement throughout the publishing process.

I must acknowledge my extended family—siblings, grandchildren, and great-grandchildren—who have provided love, laughter, and countless memories that have enriched my life immensely. Your support and understanding have been a cornerstone of my resilience.

My church family deserves special mention for being my community of faith and fellowship. Your prayers, support, and unwavering love have seen me through my lowest points and have been a bedrock of joy and celebration.

To all my friends, especially those who have stood by me through thick and thin, your companionship and prayers have been a source of comfort and strength. I am blessed to have each of you in my life.

Lastly, I thank anyone who has been a part of my journey, whether mentioned in these pages or not. Each interaction has shaped me and helped mold the chapters of my life into a story of triumph and testimony.

Thank you all for being part of my story.

About the Book

"Gloria Jean Hobbs-Thomas: Triumph Over Tragedy" is a profoundly moving memoir that chronicles the incredible journey of a woman who overcame immense adversity through faith, resilience, and the transformative power of forgiveness. In this inspiring narrative, Gloria shares her life story—from a challenging upbringing in Cedar Hammock, Florida, filled with abuse and neglect to her profound spiritual awakening and the healing that followed.

This book is more than just a personal recount; it serves as a beacon of hope for those facing trials and tribulations. Gloria's experiences with spiritual abuse, poverty, bullying, and recovery from substance abuse are laid bare, not just to tell her story but to guide others through their processes of healing and self-discovery.

Through her powerful testimony, Gloria aims to reach a diverse audience that includes incest survivors, spiritual seekers, recovering addicts, and anyone grappling with past traumas. Her message is clear: no matter the depth of despair, redemption is within reach for those who seek it, and a new horizon awaits those willing to embrace God's love and mercy.

Structured to resonate with those who need it most, the book delves into practical lessons on overcoming personal demons, embracing community support, and finding strength in faith. Gloria's narrative reminds us that healing is a journey, not a destination, and anyone can overcome the odds and emerge stronger and more fulfilled with faith, a supportive community, and inner strength.

This memoir recounts a life of overcoming challenges and serves as a spiritual guidebook for navigating the complexities of life with grace and unwavering faith. It is a must-read for anyone seeking to transform pain into power and despair into purpose.

Introduction - The Dawn of Hope

The start of my story would never be confused with some fairytale. You know, the ones about two people who fall madly in love and live happily ever after? It would be considerably more accurate to describe my parents as "entangled" than in love. My father, Robert Hobbs, and my mother, Doreatha Long, lived in a small town called Lake Butler, Florida. At my conception, my father was married to another woman with whom he had already started a family. As it turned out, my mother had a bit of a pattern of being "entangled" with men who were committed elsewhere, as my siblings had similar starts to their own stories.

As though it was not enough that I would grow up without my father, the universe saw fit to throw another curve ball my way as soon as I made my debut into the world. I was born prematurely and in need of extensive hospital care. As you can imagine, as a single mother with other children to care for, my mother had little financial resources and a growing hospital bill. Although she attempted to work with the hospital, they did not sympathize with her plight as she had hoped. Six months into my stay, I was finally strong enough to leave, but they refused to release me due to the outstanding bill.

All my mother could think of was calling my grandmother for help. Coincidentally, my grandmother did not have the means to pay the bill either. She attempted to talk to the hospital staff to work out an agreement, but they could never come to one. My grandmother walked out of the billing department with her head held high, right into my room, and plucked me out of my tiny crib. She swaddled me carefully before walking right out of the front door with me tucked away in her coat.

My "great escape" earned me a nickname and two birthdays, as it turns out. From that day on, I was known as "peanut" because I was small enough to fit into my grandmother's coat without anyone noticing. I was always told that my birthday was June 5, 1957, and all of my schools listed my birthday on that day. However, when I was ready to get married, I retrieved a copy of my birth certificate, which read, "December 9, 1957." It was as if I did not exist for my first six months of life. Since my family did not have the means to pay my bill, I was not important enough to have my birthday recorded correctly. The story of my birth turns out to have foreshadowed the themes of rejection that would repeat throughout my life.

Growing up as a 'preemie' brought its set of challenges; to this day, I wrestle with health issues. Many stem from the echoes of my mother's hardships. Like a haunting family legacy, she lost her first child that she had when she was just 16 years old, the same age I was when I gave birth to my son. Similarly, her mother had her at 16. The cycle of young motherhood brought with it the burdens of a hard life—after losing her firstborn, my mother turned to alcohol, spiraling into addiction. I'm not sure how long my parents were together, but they had parted ways by the time I was three or four. At that time, a man named Charles entered the picture, and we moved to Tampa.

Here begins my story, marked by instability and hardship but also imbued with hope and resilience. My life has been a rollercoaster of trials and transformations. Yet, through faith, perseverance, and embracing a loving community, I found the strength to rise above my past and step into a life of purpose and service.

I invite you to walk with me through these pages. I hope to lift others who face similar battles by sharing my journey. It is never too late to alter the course of your life. This isn't just my tale—it's a universal message of hope, resilience, and the unyielding power of faith.

The Seeds of Turmoil

Chapter

1

Gloria's Grace

"The gem cannot be polished without friction, nor man perfected without trials."

— Chinese Proverb

My memory reaches back to when I was about three or four years old, a time shrouded in the shadows of my early childhood in Lake Butler. Before then, the details of my life remained hidden, a gap filled only by the stories others have told.

The years of living with my mother, her friend, and my brother Alexander were marred by the echoes of loss and survival. Alexander, only a few years older than me, became my guardian in a world where our mother struggled daily with the haunting grief of losing her eldest son. Her childhood was tainted by pain and hardship, which left her lacking the necessary tools to cope with the grief she faced daily. A problematic childhood seemed like a generational curse, casting a long shadow over our family. Under constant threat of being engulfed in its darkness, we seemed to scrape by day to day, reaching for a bit of light wherever we could.

As a little girl, I faced the harsh realities of scarcity—never having enough food or clean clothes. My brother did his best, but we were just children, existing in a constant state of survival. Our lives were filled with neglect, which required learning to navigate difficulties with little understanding of our circumstances.

When we moved to Tampa, we lived in a large white house with creaking stairs that groaned and squeaked loudly, making the house seem scary and alive somehow. That house often felt more like a battleground than a home. My mother's friend would come home weary from work, only to be met with the day's failures, either by my mother, brother, or me. Voices would eventually escalate into arguments that frayed us. Some nights, the noise from the arguing seemed to battle with the house settling as if there were a prize for the one that terrified us the most.

Eventually, overwhelmed by her inability to cope, my mother made the heart-wrenching decision to send Alexander and me to live with our aunt and uncle in Cedar Hammock. I remember the tearful goodbye, the promises of return, the feel of her arms tight around us—one last embrace filled with hope and despair.

The word 'heartbroken' wasn't in my young vocabulary, but its meaning coursed through me, a sharp, relentless ache. I felt abandoned, though I wasn't alone. My aunt, related by blood, and my uncle, her third husband, took us in. Their home wasn't the refuge I hoped for; it was yet another battleground to face, as if Alexander and I were soldiers away at war.

My aunt, hardened by her abusive past and a tough life working in the fields, was not the nurturing figure I needed. She escaped into her labor, leaving me, too young for school, to tag along. Together, we toiled under the sun, picking peppers and cucumbers from dawn till dusk. Home life was just as demanding. Fetching water and preparing meals, I did my best to ease her burden.

My distant and stern uncle made no secret of his resentment toward us. "Why did you get these kids? We can barely take care of ourselves." His words stung, deepening the sense of feeling unwelcomed.

Despite the hardships, there were small mercies. Uncle Alfred, though mostly withdrawn into his work at the smokehouse and the fields, managed a farm that provided most of what we ate. I found a peculiar joy in the simple tasks like feeding the hogs and savoring the taste of fresh bacon.

We lacked the comforts of modern life. Up until I was twelve, there was no electricity. The house was neither shielded against summer's sweltering heat nor winter's biting cold. One winter, the cold became unbearable, reaching beneath my layers of clothing and gripping my bones tightly. I remember trying to light a fire in the stove to warm us, and the flames leaping out unexpectedly, scorching my face. It felt as though a thousand searing hot needles pierced my skin all at once as immense heat coursed through my face. Tears flowed as the swelling set in, and the pain morphed into a steady throb. My Uncle Bubba, my aunt's brother, became my saving grace, insisting that I be taken to the doctor. This kindness has stayed with me throughout my life and surely saved me from worse scars.

Living with my aunt, surrounded by family yet isolated by secrets and lies, I learned the harsh lessons of our family's history. The silence that enveloped our deepest pains felt like a heavy chain, one I was determined to break. Secrets, unforgiveness, and the remnants of past sins would not define my future.

Reflecting on those early years, I see a tapestry of resilience woven through the trials. Each thread is a story of survival and lessons in endurance. My journey through these memories is not just a recounting of hardships but a testament to the strength found in faith and the possibility of forgiveness. God's presence was a quiet constant, a promise of redemption slowly unfolding.

Gloria's Grace

Prayer

Heavenly Father,

In our beginnings, where turmoil often plants its seeds, we seek Your presence and peace. We acknowledge the struggles and scars that early hardships imprint upon our spirits and humbly ask for Your healing touch upon these tender wounds.

Lord, guide us through the memories that may cause pain and help us see them through Your eyes—not as permanent marks of defeat but as opportunities for growth and grace. Grant us the courage to face these challenges, trusting that You are with us, transforming our turmoil into triumph.

In Jesus' name, we pray, Amen.

Gloria's Grace

Reflections of Your Journey

1. Reflect on a time from early childhood that feels shrouded in mystery or filled in by others' stories. How has this shaped your understanding of your personal history and identity?

2. In what ways have you experienced or witnessed generational challenges within your own family? How have these challenges impacted your life choices and perspectives?

3. Can you recall a time when scarcity or hardship was a daily reality? How did you cope with these challenges, and what strengths did you discover in yourself during this time?

4. Reflect on a significant move or transition in your life. How did this change impact your sense of stability?

5. Can you remember someone who extended unexpected kindness to you in a difficult time? How did this affect your situation or how you view kindness today?

Gloria's Grace

Affirmations to Live By

1. I embrace my past as a testament to my strength and resilience.

2. I am capable of overcoming adversity with grace and courage.

3. My journey is filled with lessons that cultivate my growth and faith.

4. I am more than my circumstances; I am a survivor who keeps moving forward with hope.

Notes

_____

_____

_____

_____

_____

_____

_____

_____

Lost Innocence

Chapter 2

Gloria's Grace

"No one loses their innocence. It is either taken or given away willingly."

— Tiffany Madison

From my earliest memories, I've always felt a deep connection to something greater than myself—a constant presence I later understood as God. Growing up, Sundays were a respite, a day when we would attend church, and I'd feel aligned with this higher power. However, the rest of the week contrasted sharply, filled with the harsh reality of my uncle's disdain for my brother and me and his unkind words constantly echoing through the house.

Aunt Fannie, despite her tough exterior, was the one who introduced us to prayer. She often said, "There is a God somewhere." Whether intentional or not, in those moments, she instilled in me a hope that seemed distant amid our daily struggles. As I grew older, I understood that her stern manner was shaped by her difficult upbringing, not by any malice toward us. She shared snippets of her childhood with me—how her mother, of Native American descent, and her black father struggled, often leaving her and her siblings to fend for themselves. This revelation softened my feelings towards her as I recognized our shared battles against the scars of our past.

Aunt Fannie, childless herself, became a mother figure to many other children, stepping in whenever someone needed help. Her life had hardened her, but beneath that, she had a caring heart battered by the suffering she had faced.

Gloria's Grace

When I turned six, she enrolled me in an all-black school in Webster, where I met Miss Johnson, my first-grade teacher. She taught me to write my name and tried relentlessly to teach me to hold my pencil "properly," but to her dismay, those lessons were to no avail.

School was a mixed experience for me. I enjoyed learning, but it was overshadowed by bullying from older students, spurred on by the head bully. It took me years to learn to stand up for myself and to understand that I had the right to protect myself. In school, I met Deborah, who became my lifelong best friend.

When my brother, Alexander, was thirteen, he left my aunt and uncle's home. Around the same time, my uncle passed from his many battles with his health. His illness eventually led to his leg being amputated. Being incapacitated, forced away from his work and beloved garden, he spent his last days drinking, locked away in his smokehouse. When he passed, Aunt Frannie found herself widowed for the third time; this, along with Alexander leaving, plunged my aunt into depression.

Feeling alone, my mind drifted to thoughts of leaving my aunt's home as my brother had. My father lived close by with his family and I allowed myself to imagine him coming and swooping me away into a better life. He made no attempt to include me in his life before and asking him to take me away proved futile. Knowing he was living happily with his family, and choosing to ignore my existence deepened my feelings of resentment and isolation.

Gloria's Grace

This feeling of betrayal was compounded tragically when my brother morphed from my protector into someone from whom I needed protection. At one time, we suffered together, navigated a life we barely understood, and survived together. I trusted him unequivocally, and all was lost in one fateful afternoon. The innocence of my childhood was forever lost beneath our house that day. I took his hand, entering that crawl space as a neglected little girl who was a little broken and emerged wholly shattered. I was too young to process what happened, but that did not halt the shame, confusion, and secrecy that engulfed me.

Even now, the pain of those memories lingers, a stain on my spirit that I struggle to cleanse. My brother passed away at a young age. He lived a turbulent life that ended in mysterious circumstances. The details have never fully emerged, but it's believed that he succumbed to injuries sustained by police during an arrest. His death marked a painful punctuation to his troubled existence, reflecting the cycle of despair that plagued our family.

Gloria's Grace

<u>Prayer</u>

Dear Lord,

We come before You seeking restoration and peace. As we revisit these times of vulnerability and hurt, wrap us in Your comforting embrace, shielding us from the lingering pain of past traumas.

Help us to forgive those who have wronged us, not through our strength but through the power of Your boundless grace. Teach us to release the burdens of anger and bitterness, replacing them with Your love and understanding.

As we heal from these wounds, let us become beacons of hope and resilience for others who may tread similar paths. Empower us to use our voices.

Thank You, Lord, for Your unending faithfulness and for promising to restore all that has been broken. May this prayer uplift our spirits and renew our hearts in love.

In the name of Jesus, we pray, Amen.

Gloria's Grace

Reflections of Your Journey

1. Reflect on a moment from childhood when you faced significant challenges. What personal strengths did you discover about yourself during these times?

2. How has faith played a role in helping you through difficult times? Can you identify a person or a moment that strengthened your belief or introduced you to spiritual practices?

3. In what ways has your childhood affected your adult relationships? How have you worked to overcome these effects?

4. Have you ever had to forgive someone who deeply hurt you? What steps did you take to forgive, and how did it change your perspective?

5. How have you dealt with losing someone close to you, especially if that relationship was complicated? What coping mechanisms have you found to be most helpful?

Gloria's Grace

Affirmations to Live By

1. "I am stronger because of the trials I have faced, and I grow more resilient each day."

2. "My faith is a beacon that guides me through my darkest moments and fills me with hope."

3. "I have the right to protect my peace and prioritize my well-being in all situations."

4. "Forgiving others liberates me from the weight of past pains and opens my heart to new possibilities of joy and peace."

Notes

_____

_____

_____

_____

_____

_____

_____

The Struggle for Acceptance

Chapter

3

Gloria's Grace

"To be yourself in a world that is constantly trying to make you something else is the greatest accomplishment."

— Ralph Waldo Emerson

From my earliest memories, school was a battleground where I rarely felt welcomed. As a skinny, black, and poor girl, I faced relentless prejudice based on my skin color and economic status. Back then, even being skinny was looked down upon. Amidst this isolation, I found solace in Deborah Taylor, who remains my best friend. She approached me, saw past the superficial differences, and we formed a bond that has withstood the test of time.

"When I was fifteen, confined to the area around the railroad tracks near my grandmother's old house, I discovered a somber kind of freedom. A family of Indian descent had moved into her old home. The head of the household, a harsh and unkind man, lived there with his wife and their children. Not long after they arrived in Cedar Hammock, he started sexually abusing the oldest daughter. He fathered two children with her and seemed to repeat the pattern of abuse with her siblings.

After finishing my exhaustive list of chores, I was allowed to visit their home on Saturday evenings. My aunt was unaware of what was happening in their household, and I wasn't about to tell her. I gripped tightly onto any reprieve from the suffocating atmosphere of being at home.

My visits to the neighbor's house often ended in what I can now recognize as abuse. The kids would hold me down while the middle boy would try to force himself on me sexually. Conflicted and craving affection, I allowed these incidents to occur repeatedly, hoping it might somehow translate into the love I desperately sought. This pattern of seeking approval and love from the wrong places was a cycle I didn't have the tools to break. Thinking about it is hard for me, even now, knowing that sex has been a part of my life for the most significant part of it, starting with my brother at about five years old.

By the end of ninth grade, my relationship with my aunt had deteriorated to the point of no return. I decided not to return to her house after the summer break, which broke Deborah's heart. Despite living only five miles away, my father remained oblivious to my struggles. Daily, I endured a bus ride with white kids who hurled insults and threats, making school a place of torment rather than learning. However, amidst this hostility, God sent me unexpected allies—three white kids who became my guardians. They defended me against the bullies, ensuring I was never harmed under their watch. At the time, I couldn't see them as anything but a temporary shield from my pain.

Alone, I often cried, unable to show my vulnerability around my aunt, who dismissed tears as a waste. This emotional suppression has followed me into adulthood, leaving me to grapple with expressing my feelings.

During this same painful time of my teenage years, my vulnerability was exploited by an older man who promised to take care of me and offer the love I lacked at home. His words were sweet, and I hung on to every word, hungry for affection and a way out. I moved down South to live with my mom to pursue this relationship. I told her I was in love and refused to return to Aunt Fannie's oppressive home.

Gloria's Grace

Prayer

Heavenly Father,

We ask for Your divine presence to guide us. Help us understand that the acceptance of others does not determine our worth; Your infinite love and grace determine it.

Strengthen us, Lord, as we navigate the challenging waters of rejection and misunderstanding. Grant us the wisdom to see ourselves as You see us—valuable, cherished, and wonderfully made. Teach us to embrace our uniqueness and to celebrate the diversity You have created in Your image.

Thank you, Lord, for accepting us unconditionally. May we learn to accept ourselves and others, promoting unity and love as we walk in Your ways.

In Jesus' Name,

Amen.

Gloria's Grace

Reflections of Your Journey

1. Can you identify a time when you felt like you didn't belong? How did you navigate that feeling?

2. What coping mechanisms have you developed over the years when facing rejection or isolation? Are they healthy or harmful?

3. Who has been your most prominent advocate during times when you felt unaccepted? How did their support change your perspective or situation?

4. Have there been moments when you've compromised your true self to gain acceptance? How did that affect your sense of identity and self-worth?

5. Reflecting on past struggles for acceptance, what lessons have you learned that you would share with someone experiencing similar challenges?

Affirmations To Live By

1. I am worthy of acceptance and love, precisely as I am.

2. My value does not decrease based on someone's inability to see my worth.

3. I choose to surround myself with people who appreciate and uplift me.

4. I am resilient and capable of overcoming rejection and finding my tribe.

Notes

In the Arms of False Saviors

Chapter

4

Gloria's Grace

"Many are the plans in a person's heart, but it is the Lord's purpose that prevails."

— Proverbs 19:21

In my haste to mature, I started a relationship with Herbert, a man who quickly took advantage of my naivety. He was a predator, 35 years old when we met while I was just fifteen. He couldn't wait to strip away my remaining innocence, not knowing how scared I was or of the abuse I had already suffered. He fantasized about being with a virgin, but I was far from that. Our first encounter resulted in pregnancy. Reflecting on those moments, I realize that a genuine man would have pursued marriage if his love was sincere. Though some might consider it old-fashioned, I uphold the sanctity of marriage as God intended—a union between one man and one woman.

Life with Herbert brought nothing but instability. Looking back, I realize how far gone I was. In a failed attempt to escape his abuse, I tried to poison him once with rat poison, but it wasn't enough. I was isolated and shunned due to my pregnancy, I found that, although my aunt was harsh, she at least provided some stability. I remember being eight months pregnant, living in a Miami rooming house. A compassionate woman at a food pantry, recognizing my desperation, allowed me to call my father. Meanwhile, at home, Herbert trapped me in a closet, threatened violence, and prevented me from reaching out for help.

We later moved to a cramped trailer in Pompano Beach. When I went into labor, Herbert, incapacitated by a hangover, initially dismissed my pain. He eventually took me to a hospital, which redirected us to a free clinic in Fort Lauderdale due to our circumstances. Despite the staff's reluctance to treat a young, unmarried mother, I insisted on staying there. After enduring two days of labor and harsh judgments, I gave birth to my son, whom I named Mark Brown. Despite Herbert's baseless doubts about paternity, influenced by Mark's skin color, I knew the truth.

For fifteen years, I endured hurt and abuse, yet I never sought God's guidance or prayed for direction. Instead, I made impulsive decisions, ignoring my mother's warnings. She had endured a similar journey and tried to shield me from making the same mistakes. However, in my anger, I rejected her help, defiantly asserting, "You can't tell me what to do," as I desperately sought someone to offer me the love and care I craved.

Reflecting on those turbulent times, I reconnected with my sister Angela. We both endured sexual, physical, and mental abuse, and tragically, no one rescued us. Although her traumas differed from mine, her pain and anger mirrored my own. I've managed to cope better, perhaps because I hit rock bottom—a mental institution, severe addiction to crack cocaine, marijuana, alcohol, and a slew of personal demons. Our family culture dictated that personal issues should remain private, perpetuating a cycle of secrets and lies that I was determined to break. Now, in our sixties, the shadows of abuse still linger. I've found some peace, perhaps because I've faced the darkest depths. Rooted in deep-seated abandonment issues, my struggles continued into adulthood, and I often wondered if my great-grandfather's prayers for our family would truly reach God.

Gloria's Grace

Prayer

Heavenly Father,

In the journey through shadows, where false saviors linger and promises falter, guide our steps with Your unwavering light. Grant us discernment to see beyond deceptive comforts and the strength to reject those who lead us away from Your truth.

Help us to lean not on fleeting shelters but on Your eternal love, which shields and sustains. Renew our spirits, Lord, so that we may find refuge in Your grace and wisdom in Your word. May we always remember that our true savior is Christ, whose love never fails.

In Jesus' name,

Amen.

Gloria's Grace

Reflections of Your Journey

1. Can you recall a time when you looked to someone or something as a source of rescue, only to realize it was not what it seemed? How did you handle that realization?

2. What warning signs might you now recognize in people or situations that seem too good to be true?

3. How have past experiences with false saviors influenced your current relationships or decisions?

4. What steps have you taken to ensure you rely on healthy sources of support?

5. How can you strengthen your self-reliance and inner guidance to protect yourself from similar situations in the future?

Affirmations to Live By

1. I trust my intuition and wisdom to guide me.

2. My strength and resilience keep me strong.

3. Each experience strengthens my discernment.

4. I am committed to pursuing authentic, healthy relationships that nurture my growth.

Gloria's Grace

Notes

The Spiral into Darkness

Chapter

5

Gloria's Grace

"Only in the darkness can you see the stars."

— Martin Luther King Jr.

After my son Mark's birth on May 31, 1974, I realized two things. The first was that I was wrong in thinking I had ever felt love before seeing his tiny face for the first time. In my eyes, he was without flaws and undoubtedly my first love. The second realization I came to was that the man I was in a relationship with was not good for us. I reached out to my mother for help as soon as I could. Having a child in the world makes things different. From the moment he entered the world, I knew that I had to escape the abusive situation I had brought him into. Despite being young, I felt responsible for allowing myself to be mistreated by someone old enough to be my father. The stains of my time with him have been lasting. Although I have realized that all men do not have ill intentions, I continue to fight the mistrust that immediately swells within me when I see a young girl in the same room with a man.

In time, I was able to gather the resources to leave Herbert, but soon after, he found me and tried to persuade me to return. He promised me that he had changed and that things would be different. His words did not move me. I had experienced enough of his version of 'love' and refused to fall back into that trap. I moved in with my mom, her husband, my sister Angela, and our new baby sister, Linda. My mom was sober then, and she and her husband had stable jobs. They provided a new home, and life seemed stable. We lived in the small town of LaBelle, Florida, where everyone knew each other's business, and it quickly became known that I had returned without a husband.

Gloria's Grace

Despite needing her support, I felt a surge of rebellion towards my mom. I was angry at her for abandoning me during my childhood and felt jealous that she was now raising my sisters. It seemed unfair, exacerbating my pain and blinding me to the broader reality that we were all suffering. Our family had been dysfunctional for years, refusing to acknowledge dysfunctionality, instead opting to settle for leaving things unsaid.

Angela endured similar ordeals to my own, if not worse. She was molested for years by men who should have been protectors, including some who took advantage of her when my grandmother was intoxicated. Forgiveness has been a long and arduous journey for us. Angela remains trapped in emotional turmoil inflicted by those who should have been responsible adults.

For generations, my family stood by the familiar mantra, "What happens in this house stays in this house." Although acknowledging the truth can be uncomfortable and even painful, it is instrumental in preventing abuse and allowing survivors the freedom to tell their stories. Some might find it embarrassing that I choose to expose these family secrets, but my conscience and the Holy Spirit guide me. God aims to protect the innocent, and we must be the facilitators of that protection. Change comes from honesty with both ourselves and others. I am ready for the chains of abuse binding our family to be broken.

While living with my mother, my rebellious spirit reared its head, which created numerous challenges. My mom, grappling with her pain, lacked the patience to support me. I was part of a troubling legacy—like my mother and her mother before me, I was pregnant by fifteen. By sixteen, they were both struggling with alcoholism, spiraling out of control, and I began to tread that same destructive path, seeking affection in all the wrong places. Along with alcohol, I turned to men, mistaking any attention for love, not realizing that to them, I was nothing more than an object to be used for their desires.

Only in the last seven years have I experienced a healthy relationship with my husband, whom I affectionately call Honey. We prayed together and built a foundation based on mutual respect before becoming intimate. I am grateful that I learned to value myself enough to wait for marriage, a decision that has fundamentally changed my life for the better.

From 1975 to now, my journey has been fraught with challenges, but each struggle was part of a more excellent plan. Romans 8:28 says, "And we know that all things work together for good to those who love God, to those who are called according to His purpose." Before I was born, God knew the adversities I would face, but He also knew His purpose for my life would prevail.

My stay at my mom's house was brief. One evening, after I had been on a date, she insisted I come inside and say goodnight to my companion by eleven o'clock. Reluctantly, I stormed into the house, slamming the door behind me. An argument ensued and escalated. By the end, my mother was hitting me with a broom as she screamed profanities directed at me. I declared I was leaving, and she demanded I leave immediately. My stepdad asked her to wait until morning, and by the next day, I had found a room to rent.

Gloria's Grace

That first night alone, I put my son to bed and fell asleep, only to awaken to the breathing of a man looming over me. His face was concealed in the darkness, but his intentions were clear. I screamed and ran out of the room. Seconds later, realizing I had left my son behind, I paused. A young man noticed my distress and accompanied me back to retrieve my son. His kindness led him to offer us refuge at his parents' home.

We quickly became a couple, but the town's gossip soon brought challenges. A friend asked if I was intimate with my new partner, Red. I confirmed, and her concern was evident though unspoken. After a month, we moved in together, but the relationship's initial promise faded as I saw sides of Red I hadn't known.

One evening, he tearfully confessed his struggles with his identity, caught between being a man and a woman. I could not begin to understand the turmoil Red was experiencing then. Rather than trying to understand the complex nature of what he was experiencing, my instinct to fix things kicked in. In the end, I found that I was ill-prepared for such complexities.

I've often tried to control everything, a trait that has brought me much pain. Now, I strive to surrender to God's will, acknowledging that my efforts alone are insufficient without His guidance. The enemy could have destroyed me long ago without the Lord's protection.

Trying to meet Red's needs regarding his revelation proved overwhelming, and eventually, I had to leave. Once again, I found myself alone with my son, navigating life's uncertainties. I rented another room and worked as a bartender in a juke joint. I was young and tried to blend in with the older crowd by smoking cigarettes and drinking beer. One afternoon, Red appeared unexpectedly. He said he needed to talk and pleaded with me to accompany him to a back room in the juke joint. Leaving my son with a friend, I agreed to speak and followed him.

Inside the room, for the first time, I could truly recognize the distressed state Red was in. He stood before me, a shell of the man I knew; he appeared unnaturally feeble and overcome by emotion. His eyes met mine when he spoke, but he looked through me rather than at me. He had been crying before stumbling into my room minutes earlier. A voice that was broken and barely audible finally escaped from him after a few tense moments; I strained to hear him say, "You left me, and it hurt too much. I can't handle it anymore." I looked him over, concerned and unsure of what to say. As I reached for his hand, in an attempt to offer him a small measure of comfort, he revealed a gun that was tucked into his waistband. Moving his hand to the handle, he gripped it tightly, removing it from where it rested against him. Becoming more distressed, he started to yell while waving the gun around carelessly. As I thought of the possibility of my life ending right there in that room and pondered the future of my son, I realized that his threats were not directed at me. Instead, he was threatening his own life. I stood stunned and in disbelief.

My mind could not fully comprehend that this was happening before me. Shaking myself out of the shock I had been in, I looked at Red again, my eyes wide and filled with fear. As my voice trembled, I gently urged him to put the gun down, speaking more gently and calmly than I ever had. Before I could react further, the deafening boom of thunder suddenly engulfed the room. I closed my eyes tightly as unbearable ringing in my ears left me unable to hear temporarily. I was again frozen in time until the horrid *"thud"* of his body crashing into the ground was followed by the most horrific silence I'd ever experienced. Reality violently jerked me out of my state of shock once again. At that moment, I realized that it was not the boom of thunder that engulfed the room moments earlier. The horrific scene before me became forever etched into my memory as the horrendous truth unfolded. The deafening noise had been the boom of the fatal shot that Red inflicted on himself. As reality continued to set in, the room erupted into chaos as I regained my bodily function and screamed for help; people rushed in following the commotion. The air instantly filled with silent accusations as the reason for my screams became evident. No one's eyes met mine as they took in the scene. A few moments later, the police arrived, and after explaining the situation, they determined I was not at fault. That determination turned out not to be sufficient for Red's family.

I thought I knew pain and what it meant to be shattered entirely until that night. Living with the memories of seeing him lifeless on the ground and the sound of that gunshot echoing in my mind proved to be one of my toughest battles.

After that tragic night, some of his family, including his mother and others in our community, could not comprehend the pain he must have been in. Needing to make sense of his death, they sought to place the blame somewhere, and I was the target. Although feelings of unfathomable guilt crept in at times, deep down, I knew I wasn't responsible. If Red had blamed me, he could have acted violently towards me first, but he didn't. He knew that I wasn't the reason he felt trapped. It took years of counseling and a great deal of self-reflection for me to accept this truthfully.

The community's reaction only added to my pain. I was an outcast and the subject of cruel jokes whenever I entered a room. I lived in a dense cloud of shame and isolation. In the months after Red's death, my life started a further downward spiral. I tried to numb the pain with marijuana, but the numbness was never enough to soothe the pain of my trauma. I pretended that the brutal jokes and the label of a "killer" people thrust upon me didn't hurt, but they did. I masked my pain with a facade, barely managing day-to-day interactions.

Reflecting on this tragedy, I realize counseling could have steered me toward better decisions. However, each mistake has taught me crucial lessons about life and myself. My experiences have prepared me to help others avoid similar pitfalls. I could have avoided many hardships if I had fully trusted God's plan. Now, I carry a testimony of what God can achieve even amid chaos.

Gloria's Grace

<u>Prayer</u>

Lord,

In moments when darkness creeps, and the light seems distant, be our unwavering flame. As we journey through the valleys of shadows and despair, hold our hands tight and guide our steps.

Illuminate our paths with Your truth and love, offering glimpses of hope to keep moving forward. Grant us the courage to face the challenges, the strength to endure, and the faith to trust in Your promises.

May we remember that even in the darkest times, You are with us, transforming our trials into triumphs.

In Your holy name, we pray,

Amen.

Gloria's Grace

Reflections of Your Journey

1. Reflect on a period when you felt you were spiraling. What were the initial signs that things were beginning to unravel?

2. During difficult times, how do you typically seek help? Who or what resources do you turn to?

3. How have you managed feelings of isolation or hopelessness in the past? What strategies helped you through those times?

4. Looking back at your darkest moments, what lessons did you learn that you carry with you today?

5. Can you identify any turning points in your life that led you from darkness toward a path of recovery or enlightenment? What triggered those changes?

Affirmations to Live By

1. I recognize my inner strength and resilience, even during dark times.

2. I am not alone in my struggles; God is with me every step of the way.

3. I am committed to seeking light and truth, even when surrounded by darkness.

4. I have the power, through Jesus Christ, to rise above my circumstances and direct my life toward healing and happiness.

Gloria's Grace

Notes

A Glimmer of Light

Chapter

6

Gloria's Grace

"Even the smallest glimmer of light can illuminate the darkest paths. Embrace it, and let it guide you towards the life you were meant to lead."

— Author Unknown

By the age of nineteen, I turned to drugs, cigarettes, and alcohol as an escape—or so I thought. I smoked marijuana relentlessly, calling it my "medicine," convinced it was keeping me alive. When in reality, it was destroying my mind and filling me with a false sense of contentment.

As time passed, my addiction to marijuana, cigarettes, and alcohol deepened as I required increasingly more to stay numb enough to function each day. At yet another low point in my life, I allowed a man to exploit me, selling my time to other men for money—an arrangement where he controlled everything, including the finances. My life continued its downward spiral, slowly eroding my self-respect and ability to make sound decisions.

Eventually, I found myself in another relationship with a man named Mike. In an attempt to stabilize our lives, we moved frequently, but no matter where we discovered each new start, we found that we could not outrun our destructive behaviors. After a tumultuous period in Fort Myers, we returned to LaBelle, where my substance abuse worsened. Despite my pleas for divine intervention, I failed to take active steps toward recovery. Our relationship strained to its breaking point, culminating in our separation as I continued to make poor choices. I recognized the terrible example I was setting for my son, but at the time, I did not have the

Gloria's Grace

strength to pull myself out of the awful cycle I was in and continued to make a "b-line" toward rock bottom.

It was during this rock-bottom phase that my aunt requested my help due to her health issues. This opportunity for stability was quickly undermined by my addiction, which dominated my actions. Initially, I managed my aunt's finances, but soon after I began "helping", I faltered from my responsibilities by spending her money on drugs. The devastating burden of guilt that I felt from stealing from my aunt was always instantly relieved as I closed my eyes and allowed the numbing relief of the drugs to course through me.

At this point, it was evident that my addiction was out of control, and my community's concern led to intervention by the Department of Children and Families. A representative visited and assessed our grim situation. I was filled with dread at every question he asked, every note he made, and every time he walked through the rooms of our home. I followed him fearfully, straining my eyes for even the slightest glimpse at his notebook. I knew the life I was providing had not been sufficient and was under the impression that he was collecting the evidence that he needed to remove my son from my custody. However, somehow, he recognized the potential in me despite my circumstances and the unhealthy and chaotic state of my life at that time. He was able to decipher our needs and arrange for better care for my aunt while he encouraged me to seek treatment for my addiction.

Much like my Uncle Bubba did when I burned myself as a child, the representative from the Department of Children and Families became my saving grace. God sent them to show me I was not alone, even when things seemed too much to bear. The representative followed up regularly, ensuring that I had food and was pursuing help. I admitted my uncertainty about where to seek treatment. He directed me to a detox center in Fort Myers, which placed me on a waiting list. That night, I told myself I was going to get clean. I shared my revelation with others at the juke joint and faced skepticism and mockery. I succumbed to yet after a night of indulgence that led nowhere. I prayed earnestly that night and experienced a profound sense of peace—a clear sign that it was time to embrace sobriety and transform my life. Although the path forward had never been more apparent, I was not yet ready to start the journey towards it.

A visit to my father's house underscored how much life overwhelmed me. I struggled to raise my son and myself and failed miserably at both. On the day we were set to return to LaBelle, my stepmom offered my son Mark a chance to stay with her and my father, promising him a brand-new bike. Her offer gave me pause as I strained my mind to remember the last time I had bought my son a "brand new" anything. For a moment, I wondered if the marijuana use was harming my memory, causing this blankness in my mind. After a few moments, I concluded that I could not remember the last new thing I had purchased for my son because every dollar I had was reserved for funding my addictions.

Mark eagerly accepted my stepmother's offer to live with them, a huge toothy grin plastered across his face. His smile faded when his eyes met mine. It was as if he wanted to escape my parenting so desperately that asking my permission had been an afterthought. I looked lovingly into

Gloria's Grace

his beautiful, questioning eyes as I gently touched his face. At that moment, I knew I had to let him stay. I hugged my son tenderly, perhaps holding on for a little longer than usual, and gave him permission with a smile that took more effort than it should have. The realization that I was failing my son hit me violently, shattering me in a way that brought on more pain than anything I faced up to that point. His pure joy and excitement at the chance to live away from me stung deeper than the ridicule and guilt I faced after Red's death. This pain forged deep into my spirit, and I knew then that the stain it left would be permanent no matter how hard I worked to right this horrific wrong.

I watched him as his big smile reappeared, and he ran into his grandfather's arms while his face lit up brighter than I had seen it in quite a while. At that moment, I recognized that leaving him there was for the best, but that truth did nothing to ease the pain growing within my chest.

After that visit, I returned to LaBelle alone, with my spirit much more fractured than it had been before. My heart shattered more each day as the truth set in. Mark stayed behind because my father and stepmother were able to offer him more stability than I ever could. The humiliation of that thought, accompanied by the agonizing pain of my certainty of its truth, settled deep within me. Sitting in my home with only the remnants of my son's belongings and my drugs to keep me company, I found myself at one of the darkest points in my life, freefalling further into my addictions.

As my drug use escalated, my loneliness threatened to consume me. My search for love led me from one man to another, but never into a meaningful relationship where I could find genuine support. I could not even begin to understand what support I needed. I found it easier to ignore my needs and pour everything I had into others. That way, I never had to look at myself too deeply. I was far from ready to face my faults and do the work it would ultimately take to put my life back together. I pushed my pain down as deep as I could, telling myself that was the only way that I would survive. The chaotic cycle of moving from one failed relationship to the next continued for years until, one day, my father called me about Mark. He was frustrated and at a loss, as he knew the type of life I was leading, and he also understood that my son needed me. I can only imagine an attempt to pull me back from the holes I was continuing to bury myself in. My father told me that Mark was acting out and needed me. "Your son needs you." My father's words echoed endlessly in the days after our conversation. My son was not even an adult yet and was facing some of the same pain that I was. We were both living with holes in our hearts, and I inflicted the hole in his. We were both lost souls, devoid of the love that we needed to survive emotionally, simply existing in a life with no guidance or direction. I missed out on years of my only son's life. He had been growing up without me, lost and in pain due to my continual mistakes. The shame that I felt at that harsh reality was multiplied exponentially by the fact that I knew my son needed me, but at that time, I needed the drugs more.

My son Mark is turning fifty this month. He has undoubtedly suffered significantly because of my inability to provide a stable upbringing. I was a sixteen-year-old girl, wrecked by the hardships of my own life when I had him. I was utterly clueless about motherhood, with no example of a loving parent to imitate. Please do not misconstrue these truths as

Gloria's Grace

excuses for my behavior; instead, use them as pieces of my puzzle that allow you to see the complete picture. I have asked for Mark's forgiveness, and though it's been a long, arduous journey, he's starting to understand. Repairing the damage that I inflicted on our relationship requires daily commitment. Although our relationship has dramatically improved, I am fully devoted to ensuring that my son understands how much I cherish the bond that we are building. With each piece of trauma that we acknowledge, accept, and work through together, our relationship grows stronger. I pledge to my son to use whatever time I have left with him to nurture our relationship to its best potential. If any part of my past with my son resonates with you, I urge you to seek help. Many resources are available through community agencies willing to help. They do not want to see families face life's hardships alone as we did.

In time, I met Michael, who would become my second husband. I fully believed I could leave my troubled past behind me and start anew with him. Similarly to many couples, we dated and eventually moved in together, trusting that our mutual affection would be enough to sustain us. I understand now that we were ignorant of the necessity of seeking God's guidance regarding whether we were genuinely right for each other. We lived our lives moment to moment, unwisely using whatever desires arose within those moments as our guide to navigating life and our relationships.

During this time, I continued working in the juke joints, a setting Michael disapproved of due to the presence of numerous men. He urged me to find another job, which I ultimately did, but not before the strain revealed our true natures. My deep-seated desire for attention clashed with his jealousy. Despite the blaring red flags that indicated the doom of our relationship from its conception, we rushed into marriage. Our eagerness caused us to ignore issues that would rear their heads and cause more instability within the already weak and faulty bonds on which our relationship was built. I soon discovered that Michael was inclined to socialize late into the night without me, which led to perpetual arguing.

Suspicious of his late nights, I presumed infidelity. Still, I soon uncovered the truth: Michael was struggling with a cocaine addiction. I later found that he developed this habit during his military service, a part of his life I was unaware of, just as he was blind to the chaos of my life that preceded him. As crack cocaine continued to gain popularity in LaBelle, I started to become curious about the drug. I would soon find myself encouraging Michael to share his habit with me. At the start, he would continuously meet my encouragement with warnings, telling me that dabbling in crack cocaine was not what I truly wanted and that forming the addiction was not worth it.

Michael finally caved into my persistence after a few months. The first time I tried crack cocaine, the rush I felt was unlike anything I had ever experienced. All my problems melted away in an instant, and an intense euphoria wholly consumed me. As magnificent as the high felt, it was short-lived and fleeting. I was hooked instantly. No matter how much I pursued the feeling I experienced that first time, I could never replicate it. I even found myself blending it with marijuana, doing anything I could think of to experience that first high again. Before long, chasing that feeling morphed into an all-consuming obsession. Michael and I were both in full-blown addiction. Since he no longer needed to hide his need for the drug, we began doing it together, and before long, we were fully locked in the stronghold of the highly addictive drug.

Our addiction led us to move into his parents' secondary house, and we eventually moved into our place. Despite Michael's stable job, our finances were drained by my escalating drug habits—marijuana, crack, alcohol, and cigarettes. I blamed my deep descent into drug use on Michael, though in reality, I knew it was ultimately my choice. His addiction fueled his anger and paranoia. These volatile emotions unavoidably exploded into a violent episode that left me fearing for my life. My sister, who was present for Michael's outburst, called the police, which led to his arrest. His jail stay was short-lived, as his parents had the means to bail him out quickly. Despite a legal mandate to stay apart, we immediately reunited and fled town under the illusion that we could salvage our faltering relationship.

We settled in Bradenton and married, yet we made no efforts to abandon our destructive habits. The move did nothing to mend our fractured relationship or the emotional turmoil within our family. Our son, Mark, moved home, where he undeniably felt neglected. Although I remained fully consumed by substance abuse, I professed a desire to quit recognizing the state that my life was in. Still, each payday, I saw my earnings vanish into my dealer's pockets as he traded me for the poison that would ensure my return on every payday to come.

Gloria's Grace

Michael, Mark, and I returned to Ft. Myers, desperate for change, pledging a fresh start that never materialized. In time, we found ourselves back in LaBelle, still haunted by the vicious cycle we were growing desperate to escape. Even though I continued to struggle, a small voice in my head pushed me to do what I knew was right. I knew I needed to turn my life around and that it was a matter of deciding. The persistence of that small voice felt like an indication from God that there was still hope for me, a glimmer of light in the darkness constantly surrounding me.

Gloria's Grace

Prayer

Heavenly Father,

We ask for Your continued guidance as we navigate this path toward healing and redemption. Illuminate our way with Your wisdom and grace, and instill the patience to recognize Your hand in small mercies and subtle signs of progress.

Please help us to hold onto the flickers of hope, even when they seem faint. Strengthen our faith and renew our spirits so we may see every challenge as an opportunity to grow closer to You. With grateful hearts, we embrace the light You provide, trusting that it will lead us to the full brightness of Your love.

In Jesus' name,

Amen.

Gloria's Grace

Reflections of Your Journey

1. Can you recall when you first noticed a glimmer of hope during a tough period? What sparked that change?

2. How do you maintain hope when circumstances seem overwhelmingly negative?

3. Who has been a source of light in your life during dark times, and in what ways have they helped you?

4. Reflect on a time when a small act of kindness significantly impacted your outlook. What happened, and how did it affect you?

5. What practices or thoughts help you focus on potential positive outcomes when facing challenges?

Gloria's Grace

Affirmations To Live By

1. I am open to recognizing and receiving the signs of hope that appear in my life.

2. I am grateful for the people who bring light into my life, reminding me of the goodness around me.

3. Each step I take in healing is guided by a higher light, leading me toward peace and recovery.

4. I trust that even the smallest glimmer of hope can grow into a bright future.

Notes

_____

_____

_____

_____

_____

_____

The Path to Healing Begins

Chapter

7

Gloria's Grace

"Forgiving our parents is one of the deepest forms of love we can give and receive. It acknowledges that they, like us, are imperfect beings needing unconditional love. By forgiving, we open our hearts to the love we desire and offer the love they need, healing generational wounds for a brighter, more compassionate future and stronger legacy."

— Dr. Rod Cunningham

The small voice in my mind eventually began to grow. It went from something barely audible to something that was clearly guiding me. Although I had been far removed from the churches of my childhood at that point in my life, I began to pray. I prayed with sincerity, asking God to free me from the stifling power that my addictions held over me. I distinctly remember God putting a challenge on my spirit. He asked if I was ready for this new journey. Warning that it would not be easy by far. He also assured me that it was time for a real change that would move me in the direction of the life I deserved to live. One where I had a sincere relationship with God, one where I could repair the relationship with my son and watch him live the life intended for him, and one where I would have the strength to find happiness within myself. I silently yearned for these things and searched for the will to make them my reality.

Over the next few months, it became increasingly difficult to hide my actions. On one particular Friday, after Michael came home from work, he handed me money for the electric bill, stressing the urgency to have it paid as it was past due, and we were in danger of disconnecting our power. I looked him in the eyes and assured him I would handle it that day. However, as soon as he left, the weight of the money he had given me had somehow transformed into lead weighing down my pockets. The all-too-familiar desire for release into oblivion filled me. Before I could stop myself, I was on the streets, walking into the corner store that I frequented to buy drugs.

My plan was not to spend all the money Michael had given me. I only needed enough drugs to keep my nagging craving at bay. Recognizing the importance of the task I had promised to fulfill, I convinced myself I would somehow replace the portion I was spending by that night. I would not let my family down; I would make sure to have the money in time to pay the light bill. If I stuck to my plan, everything would work out fine, and Michael would never know.

Convinced that I had everything under control, I reached into my purse, separated a small amount of money from the rest, and handed it over to my dealer. I somewhat hesitantly watched the money disappear into his pocket. His hand re-emerged, holding between his fingers a little package that I knew contained the means to the release I so intensely craved. I quickly accepted the package and did the drugs immediately. Euphoria came over me like a wave, crashing into the shore of the beach and leaving quickly. I conjured up the willpower to leave that house and go back home. Finding pride in my power to leave, I told myself it was easy. I would replace the money, and Michael would never know I was there. An hour after my first visit, I again knocked on my dealer's door. Throughout the night, I returned until the money was gone entirely. As I held my last small package of

Gloria's Grace

escape in my hands, my eyes went from the package to my empty purse and back again. A painful tinge of guilt swept over me. I had used all of the money for our bill with no way of replacing it. Michael would be livid; our power was hours from being shut off, and once again, our problems were my fault. As I opened that package, did the drugs, and escaped into oblivion for the last time that night, all thoughts of the money, its intended purpose, Michael's impending wrath, my overwhelming guilt, and the threat of our power being disconnected left my mind. That familiar, comforting wave of euphoria crashed over me, and again, my problems melted away.

The next day, when the high was over and the drugs were gone, I had nothing to show for the money Michael had given me except an empty purse looking up at me and painful, heavy guilt consuming me from the inside out. At that moment, I felt less than a person, like something that was not worthy of anything. I broke down and pleaded with God to help me conquer the drug dependency that was destroying both my marriage and my life.

Sure enough, later that morning, the lights went out. I did not dare to tell Michael that I blew through the money on drugs. So, I lied. With a straight face, I told him I paid the bill as soon as he gave me the money the day before. I had no idea why our lights had been disconnected. When the utility driver arrived to disconnect our service, I continued to lie. I did my best to act outraged and confused, hoping Michael wouldn't see through my performance. "Didn't you pay the bill?" he inquired clearly confused. I claimed, "Yes, I paid it. They must be making a mistake." He asked for the receipt to prove to the workers that it had been paid. I had not planned for this request and frantically searched my purse for a non-existent receipt. It seemed God knew I wasn't ready to change, and for any level of change to happen in my life, I had to choose it. Up to that point, I had never chosen anything over drugs, and even with all the troubles I was facing, that did not change. I continued to descend deeper into the hole I seemed eager to bury myself in. The deeper I went, the harder it became to keep that glimmer of light within my vision.

The next payday rolled around, and I received my paycheck on a Wednesday afternoon. I promised myself I would not get high. I planned to cash the check and do the right thing. However, the store where I cashed my check also happened to be where I bought my drugs, which, to lessen the guilt that I felt regarding the substances, I called my "medicine." I was deceiving no one except myself. As I stepped outside, the dealer, who seemed to read my mind, stopped me and said, "I got some excellent stuff." Those words were magic to my ears. With a total disregard for the promise I made to myself and barely an ounce of hesitancy, I was off and running toward that wave of euphoria that relentlessly called to me. I did not stop until my money was gone. Feeling small and wishing that I could disappear.

Guilt flooded my body from the inside out once again. I fell to my knees as the shame caused by my lack of willpower overcame me. I was suddenly aware of the weight of my repeated failures. They had become too heavy and threatened to trap me within the darkness of my battle with addiction. This was my last chance to make a change. I strained my eyes to see the glimmer of light that always lingered above the hole I had dug myself into over the years.

Gloria's Grace

It was barely there, and I knew I had to grasp it now, or it would be gone, forever out of reach. If I did not choose to follow the light that God had given me to find my way out, I would finally succumb to the darkness. Before I realized I formed the words in my mind, I erupted in the most primal, guttural, and desperate prayer I had ever heard. I hardly recognized my voice as the words left my mouth. Tears flowed as I cried out. "God! Please take me into your arms. I give myself to your will. Help me to fight this battle, and I will do whatever it takes to free me from the hold that this addiction has on my life!"

That prayer marked a turning point. About a month later, I drove Mark to his job at McDonald's, where he was training for a managerial position—something that made me incredibly proud—the police pulled me over. After exchanging greetings, the officer told me he had stopped me because one of my taillights was out. After checking my documents, he returned and asked me to step out of the car, informing me that my license was suspended and that he had to arrest me. Tears flowed as I asked him to tell my son about my arrest, fearing no one else would bail me out. At that moment, the day that I fell to my knees and cried out to God flashed vividly in my memory. I pleaded with God to do whatever was necessary to help me break free from my destructive habits.

In the following weeks and months, my floodgates seemed to open as I couldn't stop crying. It was as if all the hurt, the insecurities, and the effects of my failures that I numbed with substances could no longer be held down. A friend insisted I needed therapy, suggesting I talk to a professional about my problems. I was raised to believe that one should only take their troubles to the Lord. I prayed hard for relief from my constant anguish. It was becoming harder to function. I could not keep my tears at bay while I worked. I was employed as a hospitality server in a hospital at the time. Eventually, my unrelenting emotional anguish became too much, and I sought help from the health department, which referred me to mental health services. The therapist I met was empathetic and informed me that while the first session was free, I'd need to pay for further visits—an impossibility given my financial situation.

My situation continued to spiral. At this point, Michael and I had gone our separate ways, and without his income, I was drowning in debt. I borrowed from anyone who would lend, which eventually led to an eviction. During this tumultuous period, a friend suggested I apply for assistance programs. The eviction gave me a slight reprieve from paying rent to sort out my affairs. Amid my already volatile financial situation, I lost my job, but after a tough battle, I managed to secure unemployment benefits. Every need I encountered managed to be met, and I fully attribute making it through that time in my life to God's divine intervention. Whenever my path started to feel unclear, I searched for the glimmer of light that God sent me in my darkest hours, and it was always there—encouraging, asking me to trust in God's plan, and faithfully guiding me. The more I leaned into the Lord and trusted his plan for me, the brighter the light on my path became.

As I leaned on the Lord to navigate the trials that I was facing, I was also learning a lesson in forgiveness. As I fought to turn my life around, I believed that I had forgiven others and started seeking forgiveness from those I'd wronged. I continued to feel a void within myself and often wondered why I was not feeling the immense relief I had been expecting to find from forgiving and asking for my own forgiveness from others. God put into my spirit that the void I continued to feel stemmed from me not forgiving myself. I had gone so far and made insurmountable mistakes, and I did not yet feel deserving. I ignored my assigned task of self-forgiveness and continued wandering in my search for a genuine connection with God and my spirituality. I continuously saw things in others that I set out to repair when the only way forward was to fix myself by offering and truly accepting my own forgiveness. My past was behind me, and God had already forgiven me. If our Lord and Savior, who had seen everything I had done, heard every lie I told and saw the humiliating layers of myself that I hid from most of the world, saw that I was fit to be forgiven, there was no justification to continue to punish myself.

In 2014, my struggles continued as I found myself homeless. I had been through more than most at this point in my life, but homelessness was a reality I struggled to accept. How could I, who had done what I could to help others, end up with nowhere to live? The sharp pain of another perceived failure began to rise within me, but it faded as I reached for the steadfast light that had always guided me. During this time, I lived with my sister Linda and her family while I waited for housing assistance. I was grateful for her hospitality but eager for my independence. Finally, I received a letter indicating that my housing application was moving forward in Arcadia, prompting a move to that county.

Gloria's Grace

During this transitional time, a friend suggested I live with her until my apartment was ready. We became roommates and often discussed various topics, including mental health. She spoke highly of her psychiatrist and recommended I seek similar help since I had been able to secure health insurance coverage.

On a Monday morning, I went to my appointment, filled out paperwork, answered questions, and handed over my insurance card and ID. The responses I gave during this session raised concerns for the doctor. When asked if I had ever considered self-harm, I admitted to having such thoughts at a shallow point after Michael had left.

The doctor decided I needed immediate help and arranged for my transfer to Riverview, a decision made without my ability to inform anyone. This was the start of 2015, and in hindsight, it was a pivotal moment in my journey, second only to my commitment to God. At first, I was not allowed to contact anyone, which was terrifying, but somehow, an unexpected peace washed over me at that moment.

Transported to the hospital by a police officer, I broke down, feeling isolated and scared. Thankfully, the officer let me use his phone to inform a friend of my whereabouts. Upon arrival, I surrendered all personal items and changed into a hospital gown. My first day in that new and chaotic environment was overwhelming. Sounds of distress seemed to engulf the entire building at times. Every time the distress from the other residents got overwhelming, and I needed comfort, I reached out for the presence of the Holy Spirit. My spirit would calm, and the comfort I sought would wash over me, assuring that God was with me.

Gloria's Grace

During my week-long stay, I didn't attend any classes initially; instead, they focused on evaluating me and starting me on medication. Each day brought new insights, and I learned the critical lesson of self-care: you cannot expect others to care for you if you do not care for yourself.

I realized I had neglected my needs, always saying yes to others at my expense. This pattern stemmed from not forgiving myself for the past abuse I endured and inflicted. At Riverview, I learned the importance of setting boundaries and the power of saying no without guilt. Self-forgiveness became a key theme of my recovery.

On the seventh day, I met with the team, who would decide whether I needed to stay longer or could go home. This meeting would determine the next steps in my path to healing.

Gloria's Grace

Prayer

Heavenly Father,

As we journey on this healing path, guide our steps with Your wisdom and grace. Let each challenge we face be a stepping stone to deeper faith and understanding.

Grant us the courage to confront our pasts and embrace the transformations You have planned for us. Let Your love be the light that guides us through the shadows of our past hurts, helping us forgive those who have wronged us and ourselves.

Thank You for Your unfailing support and for renewing our spirits each day.

In Jesus' name,

Amen.

Gloria's Grace

Reflections of Your Journey

1. Can you recall a moment when you felt you had hit rock bottom? How did you recognize that moment, and what was your turning point?

2. How have you approached asking for help or accepting support during challenging times? Are there moments when pride or fear held you back?

3. Reflect on a time when you felt a significant change was initiated by a crisis. How did this event reshape your path to healing?

4. In moments of deep despair or challenge, what practices or beliefs do you turn to for comfort and strength?

5. Think about the relationships in your life during a period of personal struggle. Who emerged as unexpected supporters, and how did they influence your journey to recovery?

Affirmations to Live By

1. Each day I choose to heal is a step towards a brighter future.

2. I embrace the lessons learned from my hardships; they are integral to my growth and resilience.

3. My challenges do not define me; they refine me, making me stronger and wiser.

4. I am worthy of a peaceful and fulfilled life, and I actively work towards creating it each day.

Gloria's Grace

Notes

Reclaiming My Life Through Faith and Forgiveness

Chapter

8

Gloria's Grace

"Faith is the bird that feels the light and sings when the dawn is still dark."

— Rabindranath Tagore

When I decided it was time to confront my addictions, my son had grown into adulthood. I made the call that would forever change my life and asked if he would drive me to Fort Myers for detox. "Are you sure, Mom?" he asked. I was more than sure—I was ready. He agreed to take me first thing Monday morning.

That weekend, I prepared for a journey of surrender, not knowing what awaited but trusting in God's plan. The morning I left for detox marks the beginning of not just a recovery but a rebirth. As I poured all my trust into God, that faithful light shone brighter, assuring me that I needed that and was on the right path.

Arriving at the detox center, I was fraught with nerves, facing the unknown and preparing to bring to light the deep-rooted scars my addiction left on my life. The intake process was rigorous. They checked my belongings, and I met with a counselor who assessed my readiness to detox. Saying goodbye to my son was painful; it underscored the reality that I had to face this battle on my own.

Over the next three days, I attended continuous meetings, received regular meals—a novelty that nourished both my body and spirit—and began to detox from the substances that had controlled my life: crack cocaine, marijuana, and alcohol. After the third day, I was initially expected to return home. Knowing that I was not yet equipped with the willpower to be close to the temptations that called out to me daily, I made an emotional plea to the staff.

In tears, I explained that I was unprepared to return to LaBelle. Being in the same space as the habits I was fighting daily was not something I was ready for. I was not strong enough this time. I refused to return to living as I had before. The staff, moved by my distress, made an exception, allowing me to stay longer. I called upon my faith more than ever, seeking Jesus' guidance to navigate this crucial juncture.

Understanding that the right mindset is crucial for recovery, I knew I had to surrender to the fight against my addictions fully. To win the battle, I had to be prepared for the fight of my life. I was ready to face the things that I forced deep inside and numbed with substances. As terrifying as it was, I was prepared to look deeply into myself. Again, my prayer to God on that fateful day that shame brought me to my knees and caused me to cry out flashed vividly in my mind. I was desperate for change and finally willing to do whatever it took to reclaim my life.

One of the staff members, Tanya, promised to find a suitable recovery program for me, recognizing my earnestness. She asked for a few days to arrange something and encouraged me to maintain my resolve. Those days severely tested my willpower, as I no longer had the structured environment of detox to support me. As I sat with myself, forced to face thoughts and feelings that had been buried, old habits threatened to re-emerge. For a second, I felt the thrum of longing for that crash of euphoria that would take everything away. In those moments, I leaned on the Lord and

Gloria's Grace

found that I had the strength to turn away from those thoughts. This revelation marked the beginning of my belief in my ability to overcome.

Soon after our conversation, Tanya connected with her friend, Sister Faye Adams, in Naples, Florida. Though the formal program at the First Assembly of God had been discontinued due to previous challenges, Sister Faye was willing to consider helping me individually.

Once again, I asked my son, Mark, for assistance. He didn't hesitate to support me, driving me to Naples, where my next chapter would begin. Upon arrival, Sister Faye explained the situation: the formal program had closed due to relapses, and the church only housed the homeless. My heart sank knowing that I needed structured support, not just shelter.

During our conversation, Sister Faye delved into my life story. I was candid about my struggles, selfishness, anger, and the deep-seated unforgiveness that plagued me. Moved by my openness, Sister Faye saw my willingness to change and decided to take a chance on helping me.

One of her first interventions was to address my smoking habit. When she learned I had just received two packs of cigarettes, she insisted they be disposed of immediately, emphasizing the church's no-smoking policy. We prayed together for strength to break this addiction, and incredibly, after that prayer, I found myself unable to smoke even one last cigarette. That moment marks the beginning of my journey toward physical and spiritual cleanliness.

Gloria's Grace

Grateful and overwhelmed by all that I had gained, I prepared to leave the premises. My son and his partner, Roxie, who had come from Hobe Sound to Naples, were my transportation. Though I couldn't contribute financially, their willingness to help spoke volumes about their love and support.

After continued discussions with Sister Faye about the depth of my addiction and the control it had over my life, it became clear that I was exactly where I needed to be. It wasn't a formal rehab facility but a place permeated with the presence of God—a sanctuary where healing could begin.

Sister Faye prayed fervently for me at the end of our intensive session. She called on God to reveal my true self and guide me towards a life filled with His grace. She prayed for deliverance from the evil that had dominated my life and expressed hope that I would not return to my destructive habits.

Sister Faye then led me to an open house for the homeless, where I could shower, eat, and rest. This act of kindness was not just physical help but a gesture of spiritual renewal, providing me with the first steps toward a new path, one paved with faith and forgiveness. For the third time in my life, I felt that someone had entered my path through the Lord's saving grace.

After settling in, I tidied up the house where I stayed with Sister Faye and another family. Despite the initial disarray, I felt compelled to clean—a trait I've held since youth, as a clean environment has always been essential to me. The act of cleaning not only improved the space but also brought me

Gloria's Grace

a sense of peace. Refreshed by a shower and nourished by a meal, I felt ready to tackle the emotional baggage I carried.

The following day, I woke with a deep sense of gratitude. For the first time in a long while, I hadn't felt the urge to smoke. I spent another day cleaning, transforming the house into a welcoming home. Sister Faye visited later to inform me about the Wednesday evening church service, which was mandatory for all First Assembly of God residents. It had been over two decades since I last attended a church service.

Sister Faye introduced me to the church's clothing closet and encouraged me to select whatever I needed. The church also provided meals and access to evening showers—a well-organized support system greatly appreciated by the community. I attended the service that evening, dressed in newly acquired clothes. The congregation was predominantly white, with about ten black attendees, but I was overwhelmed by the warm reception and the genuine kindness of everyone there.

The service was unlike any I had experienced before. Pastor Mallory and his family radiated genuine love, making me feel welcomed and valued. Unbeknownst to me, Sister Faye had discussed my situation with Pastor Mallory and the church staff, expressing her belief in my readiness for change and her desire to assist me in my journey.

The following day, Sister Faye invited me to her office and inquired about my feelings regarding my new environment. I described the peace beginning to grow within me, confidently stating that I believed I was where I needed to be. She shared my sentiments and invited me to a ladies' weekend retreat. Unfamiliar with what a retreat entailed, I learned it was a time for worship, praise, relaxation, and fellowship. Although I had no funds, Sister Faye assured me all expenses would be covered.

The retreat proved to be a revelation. We traveled together in a van, and the atmosphere was light and joyful. Upon arriving at a beautiful hotel, I recognized it as my first genuinely positive hotel experience. The first evening included a meet-and-greet and a praise and worship session. However, amidst the joy, I felt a wave of loneliness and a sharp sting of feeling out of place. Tears began to flow as these feelings overwhelmed me, but the women quickly gathered around me. They prayed fervently, rebuking the darkness threatening to creep back in and supporting me through my moment of vulnerability. Their actions reinforced the sense of community and belonging I had longed for, and I felt a powerful shift within me.

During the retreat, I noticed a young girl named Kim in a wheelchair. Despite her limitations, she praised God with enthusiasm. Witnessing her devotion, the Holy Spirit challenged me, highlighting my self-pity. Overwhelmed, I knelt, pleading for God's forgiveness and the strength to improve. I fully believed that the light I desperately clenched on to the day that I cried out to God, desperate for his divine intervention, had led me to the path I was on. During my time at the retreat, it only grew brighter, and by the end of our time there, my path forward was once again as clear as it ever had been. I fully committed my life to Jesus, asking Him to guide my daily decisions.

Gloria's Grace

At the shelter, Sister Faye, Pastor Mallory, and the staff recognized the ongoing need to support those battling addictions. They decided to give the rehab program another chance, and I became their test case. My initiative in maintaining the house impressed me, so Sister Faye appointed me the house mom. The house soon filled with women struggling with drug and alcohol dependencies.

The program's restart was challenging. Previous setbacks had left the staff disheartened, particularly after a storm-induced evacuation led to several relapses. Despite these challenges, I was determined to change. I assured Sister Faye of my commitment, which she supported through fervent prayer.

While some residents were not prepared to commit to recovery fully, a few of us sincerely wanted to change our lives. I understood where they were in their journey and refused to pass judgment because I had been in that place once. It took years of failed attempts, feeling trapped, and hitting rock bottom repeatedly. I had finally arrived at the point in my journey that I no longer wanted drugs in my life. "I DO NOT WANT TO GET HIGH ANY LONGER!" became our rallying cry and still resonates with me today. As the program expanded to include men, I faced challenges enforcing rules. Frequent visits to Sister Faye for guidance reminded me to seek solutions through prayer rather than complaints.

In my role, I had the privilege of a private room, allowing for deep personal reflection and prayer. The facility quickly reached capacity, but when a desperate young woman named Kwis arrived, claiming she had nowhere else to go, I couldn't turn her away. After praying with Sister Faye, we secured a temporary solution for Kwis, demonstrating our community's commitment to supporting each other.

Three months into my stay, I was transformed. Initially frail and indistinguishable, I began to thrive—nourished by regular meals and spiritual sustenance. I couldn't remember when I could look in the mirror and see a healthy version of myself looking back. During this period, I bonded deeply with Lisa, a fellow resident. Feeling a new comprehension of my faith, I needed to be baptized again as I could finally fully grasp God's sacrifice and love. The daily routine, including Bible study and life skills classes, taught me adult responsibilities I had never mastered. Sister Faye also instructed us on financial stewardship, which included managing our food stamps wisely.

After six months, I earned a position cleaning the sanctuary and other areas of the property. I maintained an early rising routine, allowing me quiet time with God each morning. This practice, focusing on gratitude and seeking forgiveness, fortified my recovery and spiritual growth, becoming my most significant source of strength.

My time at First Assembly was transformative, enriched by unconditional love and acceptance from people who never judged me. Although most attendees were Caucasian, Pastor Mallory emphasized their genuine respect and focus on heart changes rather than color.

The process was slow, and I was still frightened of relapsing. However, I learned to protect myself by changing my associations and habits. I surrounded myself with Christians or those aspiring to a better life, avoided unhealthy venues, and abandoned my old destructive behaviors. While I am far from perfect, my faith in God helps me make better choices.

The First Assembly of God offered me my first legitimate job opportunity, which did not involve squandering my earnings on drugs. Initially, I did not trust myself with money, so Sister Faye managed my finances. This arrangement allowed me to focus on my recovery and work without the pressure of financial management.

Sister Mallory then offered me additional work cleaning her and her mother's homes. This responsibility off campus bolstered my self-worth; I felt valued and respected, feelings I had never fully experienced before. All my prayers and reliance on the Holy Spirit were crucial during this time—they were the best things that had happened to me, aside from the birth of my son.

I fell deeply in love with God, thankful for the salvation and new life He granted me. My relationship with Him deepened significantly, affecting every decision. I yearned to return to my routine of seeking God's guidance each morning, asking Him about my daily actions, what to wear, and what to eat.

Faith was the cornerstone of my recovery at the First Assembly of God. I learned to trust in God, others, and myself—a trio of trust I had never possessed. Hebrews 11:1 became a personal testament, as the evidence of my shattered spirit seemed contrary to recovery, yet the church staff's faith painted a different, hopeful picture.

Gloria's Grace

Pastor Mallory's favorite hymn, "I Surrender All," touched me profoundly during each service. His assurance that no one could dictate another's needs from God underscored the importance of personal spiritual relationships.

From the moment Sister Faye prayed for my deliverance from smoking, and it was granted, my faith ignited. It grew as I experienced the Holy Spirit's power, elevating my faith to new heights. Philippians 4:13 resonated deeply: "I can do all things through Christ who strengthens me."

However, adjusting to this spiritual high was challenging. I had replaced my addiction to substances with what I jokingly called a 'church addiction,' desiring to stay within the church's sanctity as much as possible.

Living on the property of the First Assembly of God, I learned about Jesus Christ's unconditional love. It taught me to see myself differently, to love God first, then myself and others. This understanding of love was a revelation; I had never truly known it before my time at the property. Although Sister Faye and Kwis have since passed, their memories and impact remain firm in my heart.

Even after leaving, I occasionally return to Shadowlawn Drive in Naples, Florida, whenever I need to feel God's presence distinctly. This spot is where He performed significant work in me. At home, I have established unique places for communion with God—beside my bed, on a pillow, and at the kitchen table, where I engage in daily devotions with the Holy Spirit. These personal sanctuaries remind me of the peace and guidance I first experienced at

Gloria's Grace

First Assembly, grounding me in my ongoing journey with faith.

I had transformed so significantly at the First Assembly that people hardly recognized me as the frail woman who had first arrived. The Holy Spirit had worked miracles in my life, a change for which I am eternally grateful. My husband, Michael, noticed these changes too. He visited and joined me for a church service, impressed by my progress. Afterward, we went to lunch, reminiscing about my journey and his pride in my transformation.

During one of his visits, my sister Linda also came to see me. She was astonished at the changes in me. It was clear that the transformation God had worked in me was visible to everyone.

However, reconnecting with Michael soon turned from uplifting visits to a rekindled relationship. Despite Sister Faye's cautious advice to take things slowly, we rushed back into our relationship, convinced that my changes would suffice for both of us. We returned to LaBelle, ignoring that we were now unequally yoked—me, a fervent Christian, and him, still indulging in old habits.

Back in LaBelle, people labeled me a "holy roller" because of my newfound dedication to Jesus and the church. I was determined that my faith would shield me from surrounding evils. However, making the same mistake that we had at the start of our relationship; we didn't seek God's guidance for our lives or marriage and skipped essential steps like marriage counseling to heal from past abuses.

Gloria's Grace

Our reunion lasted about four years. Although Michael eventually embraced Christianity, the deep-seated issues from our past relationship weren't addressed, leading to frequent, trivial disputes. I pressured him to quit his vices and embrace faith as I had, which only drove a wedge between us.

One morning, the strain became too much for Michael. He tearfully declared he could no longer continue in our marriage. Despite my desperate pleas and promises to change, he was resolute. As he packed his belongings, my pain turned to anger.

That night, consumed by bitterness and thoughts of revenge, the unimaginable thought of using his pistol against him entered my mind. During a shallow moment in my life, overwhelmed by rage and despair, I drove around searching for either Michael or my dealer, whoever I could find first. My mind overflowed with thoughts of murder and relapsing into drug use. I had no room to think logically as I allowed those thoughts to envelop me. By God's grace, I found neither Michael nor a drug dealer that night. As I reflect on that night and consider the state of mind at the time, I am overwhelmingly thankful that God stepped in and did not allow me to make a decision that would either throw me back into the clutches of addiction or make a mistake that would haunt me forever.

My subsequent seven-day stay at Riverview Institution was enlightening. It taught me crucial life lessons, particularly about the dangers of being a "yes person," which had often skewed my life's balance. A counselor there reassured me, saying, "You don't belong here. You've just been making some bad choices." This affirmation helped me see that while I wasn't mentally ill, my poor decisions had consequences that mirrored those of someone who might be.

These experiences at Riverview highlighted the importance of self-forgiveness, a process I continue to navigate. Despite occasionally resurfacing regrets, the ongoing work of the Holy Spirit in me has significantly improved my well-being. I'm far healthier now than ever, learning to embrace forgiveness fully and the profound lessons it brings into my life.

As I continue my journey with God, the Holy Spirit, and Jesus Christ, I find reassurance in believing that all things are possible through them. Jeremiah 29:11 has always resonated deeply with me, reminding me that God's plans are for my good, not for harm. This scripture taught me that, although evil may still touch my life, I am equipped to combat it through Christ within me.

Post-institution, I struggled with the medication prescribed for my anxiety. While it subdued the symptoms, it left me feeling overly sedated. My therapeutic journey continued until the onset of the COVID-19 pandemic when my sessions paused. My therapist often commended my progress, acknowledging my ability to apply the coping tools we discussed.

Now, in 2024, I no longer rely on medication; my therapy comes through my faith in "Dr. Jesus." I've learned crucial life skills—setting boundaries, prioritizing my needs, and not

Gloria's Grace

attempting to fix everyone else's issues. Thanks to my divine guidance, my spiritual growth has been tremendous.

Gloria's Grace

<u>Prayer</u>

Heavenly Father,

We thank You for Your unending grace and the strength You provide on this journey of healing and forgiveness. As we reclaim our lives through the power of Your love, help us to forgive those who have wronged us, just as You have forgiven us.

Grant us the courage to face our past with faith and move forward in Your forgiveness. May our hearts find peace in Your promises, and may our spirits embrace the new beginnings You have set before us.

Strengthen us to walk in faith and love, reflecting Your grace in every step.

In Jesus' name,

Amen.

Gloria's Grace

Reflections of Your Journey

1. What are the pivotal moments in your life that have defined or redirected your path toward healing and forgiveness?

2. How have you seen faith play a role in overcoming your past struggles?

3. Can you identify a person or event that significantly influenced your journey toward recovery and forgiveness?

4. In what ways have you struggled to forgive yourself or others, and what steps can you take to begin that process?

5. Reflect on a time when you felt a transformation in your spirit. How did this change impact your relationships and self-perception?

Affirmations to Live By

1. I am empowered by my faith to overcome any adversity.

2. Each day brings a new opportunity for healing and growth in my spiritual journey.

3. I embrace forgiveness to liberate my heart and mind from past pains.

4. God's love guides me through the darkness, lighting my path toward recovery and redemption.

Gloria's Grace

Notes

Love Rediscovered

Chapter

9

Gloria's Grace

"Love is an irresistible desire to be irresistibly desired."

— Robert Frost

At Shiloh Missionary Baptist Church in Arcadia, I met my husband, Minister Ronald Thomas. We were introduced by Pastor Redmond during a Friends and Family Day service. Our connection was instant and divinely ordained. As we approach our ninth anniversary, I am profoundly grateful for a marriage grounded in mutual faith, which has taught me the true essence of being a godly partner.

Our marriage illustrates the challenges and blessings of being equally yoked in faith—a stark contrast to my past relationships. This alignment in spiritual values has been essential in navigating the complexities of marriage.

After meeting Minister Thomas, I began sharing my daily devotions with him, a practice I started in 2012 to find peace after my breakup with Michael. This routine not only brought me closer to God but also allowed me to connect with others on a spiritual level. Sherryl Cusseaux, a pivotal figure in my life, encouraged me to enhance my devotions with inspirational content and music, significantly enriching my shared messages.

One morning, after sending my devotion to Minister Thomas, his appreciative response confirmed that interactions between us had been meaningful. Our connection continued to deepen with the daily discussions regarding our devotionals. One day, he sent me a text asking if he could give me a call. That call went on to lead to our first

Gloria's Grace

date. Aware of the potential pitfalls, I sought God's guidance to ensure our date honored our commitment to faith.

On the day of our date, he visited me in Arcadia. Since the town lacked a movie theater and a mall, our outing included a simple trip to Walmart, followed by an evening watching movies at home. This simple, genuine connection underscored the importance of shared values and mutual respect in our relationship.

As our relationship progressed, there came a moment during a movie when he leaned in for a kiss. I consented, and we shared a tender moment. Yet, as he moved to kiss me again, I paused to express my thoughts. I explained that although I enjoyed our closeness, we needed to proceed with caution in our new relationship. We were Christians, and it was crucial not to rush into physical intimacy without fully understanding each other. I needed to share more about my past before we could move forward. He listened and unexpectedly proposed marriage. Shocked by his sudden proposal, I hesitated before accepting. My faith guided me despite the abruptness, and the decision felt right."

We hurried to the courthouse to apply for a marriage license. The clerk informed us of a mandatory three-day waiting period. These days were a whirlwind as we prepared to tell our families and arrange our wedding, which took place incredibly swiftly—from our engagement to marriage in just over three weeks.

Our family reactions were mixed. My new husband was a recent widower, which raised concerns among his family about the timing of our marriage. My own family was weary,

Gloria's Grace

knowing my impulsive nature. Despite the doubts, we felt supported by our faith and the Holy Spirit.

We married in a simple ceremony officiated by Pastor Redmon on Halloween. Thanks to the generous spirit of our congregation, the church community quickly put together a celebration with decorations, food, and a beautiful cake. Although leaving my church family in Arcadia was difficult, the night was filled with joy and love.

The evening ended with us heading to Tampa, my new home. During the drive, we discovered more about each other, and I felt reassured of our shared commitment to this new chapter. As we discussed our future, we laughed and sang, celebrating our union and the unexpected blessings it brought.

Reflecting on our whirlwind romance and wedding, I'm truly grateful for the divine guidance that brought us together. It's been a journey of learning and growing together, loving God and each other, and embracing the life we've built. Our marriage is a testament to the power of faith and God's grace in guiding us to find each other at the right time.

Our family includes eight children from previous relationships, about twenty-four grandchildren, and eight great-grandchildren. My parents have passed, but Honey's 97-year-old mother is a vital presence in our lives. I regard her not as a mother-in-law but as a second mother, a blessing from God who enriches our family with her wisdom.

In this new chapter of my life with Ron, we fondly refer to each other as Honey. Reflecting on these past seven and a

Gloria's Grace

half years, I see that God prepared me to be a wife, mother, daughter, sister, aunt, and devout Christian. I am immensely grateful for Ron's companionship; he treats me with profound respect and affection, affirming me as his queen.

Since marrying Honey, I've experienced many firsts: my first honeymoon on a cruise, horseback riding, and even holding a baby alligator during a zoo visit—fearful yet brave moments captured in photos as proof of my newfound courage.

Like any marriage, ours faces challenges, but we've learned to approach conflicts with love. One night, a disagreement escalated, and in anger, I packed my bags and left, thinking I needed space. I checked into the Holiday Inn Express, a place I was familiar with from my time as a breakfast cook. As I showered away my tears, I realized I was spiraling into old, destructive patterns.

Not long after settling in, Honey called. Within minutes, he was at my door, ready to talk. He convinced me that separation wouldn't solve our problems. We needed to face them together. So, we packed up my things, checked out, and returned home to discuss and pray for our relationship's longevity.

This moment represented the first instance that illustrated the importance of trusting my husband's wisdom. In that moment, he not only showed me the importance of communication, but he also showed me that I do not have to fall back into old patterns. He made me feel safe enough to express myself instead of pushing my feelings inward as I had become accustomed to doing. Later in our marriage, my trust in his wisdom quite literally saved my life. He insisted on medical attention for a sharp abdominal pain I had been experiencing. Through that medical attention, an intestinal issue was uncovered and treated.

Deacon Washington, a church member, often reminds us that despite life's challenges, our union is blessed and strong enough to endure. His resilience is a lesson for us all. Similarly, Honey has been my anchor, particularly in overcoming my fears, which are significant hindrances in my life. He reminds me, "Fear is of the devil, and God does not give us a spirit of fear." His support has been instrumental in my journey toward fearlessness. This journey underscores the profound ways God shapes our paths, preparing us for roles we could scarcely imagine. I am continuously thankful for His guidance and the life I share with Ron, built solidly on our faith and mutual love for each other and God.

Gloria's Grace

Prayer

Heavenly Father,

Please bless our hearts with the grace to love authentically, embracing the joys and the trials that come with deep affection.

Strengthen our relationships through Your wisdom, and let Your love be the cornerstone of our interactions.

Help us to cherish and honor the love rediscovered in our journey, and may it glorify You in every shared moment.

In Your holy name, we pray,

Amen.

Gloria's Grace

Reflections of Your Journey

1. Have you ever experienced a renewal or rediscovery of love in your life? What did that feel like, and how did it change your perspective?

2. What role has forgiveness played in your relationships? How has it helped or hindered your growth with others?

3. How do you balance the need for personal space and the desire to resolve conflicts in your relationships?

4. Can you think of a time when a relationship challenged your values or beliefs? How did you navigate that situation?

5. Reflect on a moment when someone else's faith or spiritual journey deeply influenced your own. How did it impact your life choices?

Affirmations to Live By

1. I am worthy of giving and receiving love that respects and honors my spiritual journey.

2. Each day offers a new opportunity to strengthen my relationships through understanding, patience, and forgiveness.

3. I am grateful for the people who challenge me to grow in love and faith.

4. My heart is open to transformative experiences that deepen my connections and enrich my spiritual walk.

Gloria's Grace

Notes

A New Horizon

Chapter 10

Gloria's Grace

"Every new beginning comes from some other beginning's end."

— Seneca

My early life was undoubtedly a struggle, but now, I'm on a new journey that allows me to use my past struggles to help others. The work of the Holy Spirit in my life continues to be awe-inspiring. He's healing every broken place within me, reassuring me that it can be done for others.

I will forever be thankful to the Lord Jesus for choosing me to have the strength to turn my life around and overcome the darknesses that were a part of my life for so long. I share my story openly so that perhaps someone reading this will be inspired and realize that though they may be in a dark place at that moment, it does not have to be forever. I want people to know that every life has the potential to be beautiful. It requires work on their end and believing and trusting in the Lord through every struggle.

Although my life has changed for the better, at times, I still feel overwhelmed. In those moments, I find solace in Psalm 23, reminding myself, "The Lord is my Shepherd; I shall not want"—not for anxiety, fear, or anything contrary to God. Now, as a living testament to God's power, I see how He's continuously working in me, shaping me into His likeness. What a mighty God we serve!

My relationship with God is my top priority today, followed closely by my husband, family, and friends. I'm fortunate to have so much love and prayers surrounding me. I cherish the mornings spent in devotion, sharing one-on-one time

Gloria's Grace

with the Holy Spirit, praying with my husband, and discussing God. What a blessed life I lead! And let's not overlook the joy of spending time with our precious grandson. When I had my son, I was in a difficult place. I didn't understand how to be a good parent, so God granted me a second chance with our grandson. Thank you, Lord.

My relationship with my son has improved significantly. Writing this book has allowed me to view his struggle with forgiving me in a new light. I used to hope for his immediate forgiveness without understanding that forgiveness is a process, especially for deep hurts. Reflecting on my life during these past five months, I have acknowledged the chaos I caused in his life.

My life experiences have taught me that forgiveness isn't always instantaneous. It's a journey, particularly when the hurt runs deep. I pray that God assists me and others on this journey of forgiveness. The most profound lesson in my journey has been that when we let go and let God lead the way, the beautiful life God has intended for us will shine through.

Gloria's Grace

Prayer

"Heavenly Father, as we step into this new horizon, we ask for Your guidance and light to pave our path. Please grant us the courage to embrace the changes and challenges that come with new beginnings.

Bless us with wisdom to learn from the past and hope to move forward with faith. Help us see each new day as an opportunity to grow closer to You and use our experiences to help others find their way.

May this new chapter be filled with Your grace and peace, showing us and those around us Your endless possibilities.

In Jesus' name,

Amen."

Gloria's Grace

Reflections of Your Journey

1. In what ways have you experienced transformation in your own life that you once thought impossible?

2. How do you perceive the role of adversity in shaping your character and faith?

3. Can you identify a time when a perceived setback was a setup for a greater blessing in your life?

4. How have your past experiences equipped you to help others facing similar challenges?

5. What new horizons are you approaching, and how are you preparing to meet them with faith?

Affirmations to Live By

1. I am open to new beginnings and trust that God's plans for me are for my good.

2. Every challenge I face is an opportunity to grow closer to God and deepen my faith.

3. I am a living testimony of God's grace and redemption, inspiring others through my journey.

4. With each new day, I am empowered to live a life filled with purpose and guided by divine wisdom.

Gloria's Grace

Notes

A Love Letter to My Legacy

Chapter

11

Gloria's Grace

Legacy of Love Letter to My Great Grandchildren's Grandchildren

Year 2075

Dear Beloveds,

As I write this letter, the world around us looks much different than it will when you read this in 2075. My heart swells with hope and prayers that these words find you in a time of peace, love, and enduring faith. Although I will not meet you in this life, I am confident that our spirits are connected through the family bond and the ever-lasting love of God.

Throughout my life, God has been my cornerstone, guiding me through every challenge and blessing me in countless ways. My journey has been one of transformation, shaped by my unwavering faith in God's plan and promise. It is this faith that I hope to pass down to you, my precious future generations.

Know that I love each of you deeply, even those I have not seen with my earthly eyes. You were in my heart when I wrote my book, Gloria's Grace: Triumph Over Adversity. I penned each word with the prayer that it would reach the generations, touching your hearts and guiding you towards a life full of grace and purpose.

In my story, you will find lessons of resilience, the power of forgiveness, and the boundless strength that faith can provide. I sincerely wish you to live an extraordinary, fulfilled Christian life, walking steadfastly in the path of righteousness.

Gloria's Grace

May you always turn to God in times of need and celebration, just as I have, and find comfort in His eternal presence.

As you navigate your journeys, remember where we come from—a lineage strengthened by faith and love. Let these be your guiding stars, leading you to make choices that honor our family's legacy and your relationship with the Lord.

May your lives be a testament to the faith that has sustained me, and may you pass on this legacy to the generations that will follow you. Stand firm in your beliefs, cherish each other as I cherish you, and always extend grace as generously as our Savior has given us.

With all the love my heart can hold,

Gloria Jean Hobbs-Thomas

Conclusion

Gloria's Grace

My faith in God has reached new heights. Although I don't have everything figured out, I'm content with where God has placed me. I know He shapes my heart to forgive and trust in Him fully. Learning to listen more and speak less is a challenge, and daily, I seek the Holy Spirit's assistance to overcome the impulses of my flesh. While I aim to support others, I am reminded that God also works on me.

God introduced this book into my life at a pivotal moment, forcing me to confront my past and cultivate compassion for others. We all carry past burdens we aren't proud of, but how we live today matters. Are you dwelling in past pains, or are you walking in the forgiveness and grace of God, allowing yourself to form a new testimony? God taught me to respect myself enough not to let others misuse or abuse me.

Satan uses those who would exploit a generous heart to derail you from God's plans. Wisdom and discernment are crucial to prevent such exploitation. Sometimes, I manipulated others without remorse, lost in my sin. But now, empowered by the Holy Spirit, I am quick to repent if I falter because the Holy Spirit nurtures growth and maturity in us each day.

We must embrace growth and learn to be content, understanding that joy comes from God. "This is the day the Lord has made; we will rejoice and be glad in it" (Psalm 118:24). Holding onto bitterness and unforgiveness stunts our spiritual growth, while forgiveness, though challenging, is essential for walking with Jesus.

Gloria's Grace

Thank you, Jesus, for the journey of my life. As a child, I constantly questioned my difficult circumstances—why the absence of parents, why the abuse, why the discrimination? Now, I understand that all my trials serve to reveal God's glory. In John 9:1-12, Jesus says that a man's blindness was meant to display the works of God, not because of sin.

My experiences, as harsh as they were, were meant to showcase God's power throughout my life. Now, understanding my purpose, I embrace who I am: redeemed, loved, and filled with the Holy Spirit. These truths fortify me against depression and despair because, as John 3:16 states, "For God so loved the world, that He gave His only begotten Son, that whosoever believeth in Him should not perish, but have everlasting life."

Reflecting on my life, I see it as the beginning of what God intends to do. He has been preparing me for greatness, which started with buying a computer to learn how to use it. This memoir is part of that preparation, shedding light on the darkest parts of my past and offering hope to others.

Forgiveness is a significant theme in my journey—it's necessary for moving forward. Whether forgiving others or myself, it's a continuous process that requires divine assistance. This writing journey has been transformative, allowing me to confront and forgive, finding peace and a deeper connection with God.

In summary, my life's story is a testament that no matter how low you fall, turning to God can lead to redemption and a life filled with purpose and joy. God's plans are perfect, and

Gloria's Grace

all things are possible through Him. Thank you for sharing in my journey.

Made in the USA
Columbia, SC
14 December 2024